JUDGMENT

THE BOOMERANG EFFECT

DICK SORENSON

Compiled by
DONNA SORENSON AND TAMI SORENSON
GAUPP

Illustrated by
BECKY HANSEN

THE LANYAP LIFE BOOKS

Copyright © 2019, 2022 The Lanyap Life Books

All rights reserved. This book or any portion thereof may not be reproduced or used in any manner whatsoever without the express written permission of the publisher, except for the use of brief quotations in a book review.Unless otherwise stated, all scripture quotations taken from the New American Standard Bible® (NASB), Copyright © 1960, 1962, 1963, 1968, 1971, 1972, 1973, 1975, 1977, 1995 by The Lockman Foundation. Used by permission. www.Lockman.org

PRINT ISBN: 9781736113998

eBook ISBN: 9798985927726

1116 Vista Avenue #353, Boise, Idaho 83705

www.thelanyaplife.com

CONTENTS

How to interact with this material   5

1. Judgment   9
2. A Lesson I Will Never Forget   15
3. Scriptures to Know   31
4. The Boomerang of Judgment   43
5. Action Steps to Freedom   51

About the Author   55
More Topics in This Series   59
Special Thanks   65
Other Books   67

HOW TO INTERACT WITH THIS MATERIAL

Our suggestion to you, as you read this material, is that instead of trying to search your memory and recall events or incidents in your life that the topics in *Journey to Wholeness* could apply to, pray this simple prayer:

> Lord, I thank you that my life belongs to you. All the restoration that you plan to do in my life is in Your hands. Holy Spirit, I give You permission to bring any and all events and situations to my mind that You want to heal and restore.

> *As Psalm 23:3 says, "He restores my soul; He guides me in the paths of righteousness for His name's sake."*

How to interact with this material

As He is leading, receive the restoration that happens as He helps you apply the principles in this series. Record the specifics of this restoration process. This will be your testimony of God's goodness and faithfulness to provide all of your needs. As He leads, you can share this testimony of God's miraculous provision with family and friends so God can use and bless it for generations.

Hiking toward hope on a personal journey to wholeness…

How to interact with this material

A message to you from Dick --

> This series is called *Journey to Wholeness* because it is the journey the Lord is taking me on to become whole. I find it has changed me and will do the same for others. I would say, as you discover these truths, take time with the Lord and ask Him to give you revelation on how to apply these in your own life. This is great preparation for ministering to others and training others to minister.
>
> May God guide and bless you as we journey together with Him. Welcome to The Journey!
>
> —DICK SORENSON

Welcome fellow travelers on our journey to our inheritance as His sons and daughters!

CHAPTER 1
JUDGMENT

There is an old saying that says, when you spit into the wind – you get a wet face. The scripture says if you judge – it will come back upon you.

Thus: The Boomerang Effect.

Image 1: The Boomerang Effect

This is the topic we will explore. We are not called to be everyone's critic; we are called to love one another and give mercy and grace.

Judgment is important; as a matter of fact, it is inevitable. We are often told to have good judgment and not bad judgment. Most of our training in life has to do with judging whether things are good, bad, right, or wrong. Much of our education is based on searching and researching to find what works and what does not work.

Life is a constant process of deciding and evaluating circumstances, actions, and words. We make decisions and life-choices based on the information we have and our evaluation of that information. We then make our plans accordingly. So, in this life, it is very natural and automatic to judge. Indeed, it seems necessary. But is it?

In the first two chapters of Genesis, after God created all things, including man and woman, there was no judgment. Instead, man and woman experienced open, intimate, transparent fellowship with God and each other. Man was learning, receiving, and experiencing truth from God and with God.

So, mankind's decisions, actions, and motives were based on their relationship with God, and His impartation of truth and understanding. It is much like a father and mother do with their children. They give them more factual information and experiential knowledge based on the parents' understanding of their children's ability to comprehend and apply the new information (so timing is always an important factor).

In the third chapter of Genesis, we see accusations (an evil report) and judgment introduced by Satan. He did this by asking questions that inferred a negative motive about God and His Fathering relationship with mankind. The suggestions were partially and factually true, but the overall intention and motive were false and deceiving.

When mankind entertained and accepted Satan's deceptive information, he changed the relationship with his Father. Then, man began to relate to his Father based on his own knowledge of good and evil (right and wrong), and not rely on the trusting, intimate, transparent fellowship he previously experienced. From that time on, mankind's judgment ruled, and everyone did what was right in their own eyes. (Judges 21:25)

What is Judgment?

- To pass a sentence.
- To condemn.
- To evaluate or conclude according to our view of justice.
- To form an opinion based on the law.
- To establish the truth.
- To make a final decision as to the truth.
- To throw away or destroy.

Image 2: When We Judge-God the Father Becomes Our Judge

Judgment means to pass a sentence, to condemn, to evaluate, or come to a conclusion, according to your view of what is just. It is your opinion, based on your understanding of the law, to establish the truth. It means to come to a final decision as to what is the truth; to throw away or destroy. All of this addresses judgment.

If we are judging, then the end result is that God the Father has to relate to us as our Judge instead of our Father.

Judgment

Image 3: We Ask Questions to Reach a Verdict

How We Judge

- Ask questions
- Investigate
- Evaluate
- Analyze
- Discern
- Appraise
- Recognize
- Conclude
- Pronounce

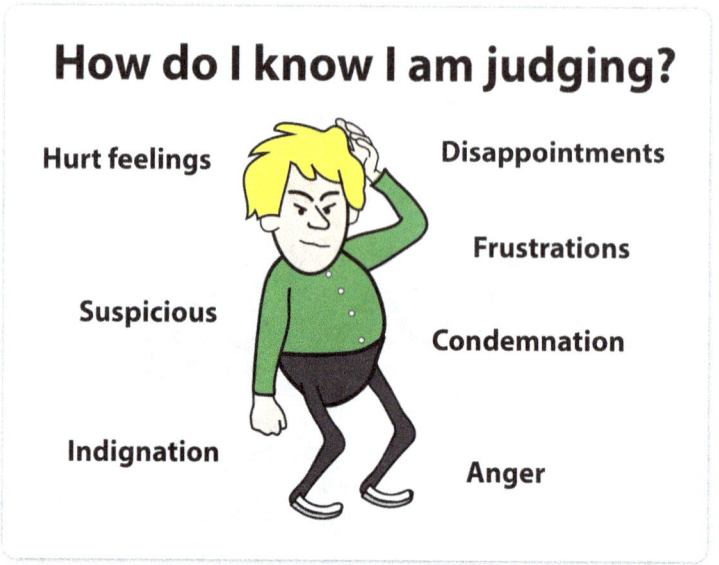

Image 4: Ways to Know We're Judging

Our judging produces more judgment in those around us.

Sowing judgment produces more judgment which is multiplied in our community. Instead of mercy and grace, criticism and discord are spread. And we experience more separation in our lives.

I previously did not spend much time thinking about judgment. This was something I had to learn the hard way.

CHAPTER 2
A LESSON I WILL NEVER FORGET

*L*et me tell you the story of what God taught me. Our son, Rick, was moving to Boston to go to an Art University. Donna and I were flying from the western part of the United States to spend time with him in Boston, before going to Portugal and other areas of Europe to minister for three months. After we helped Rick move into his apartment, we took him out to lunch.

While we were eating, Rick said, "Dad, let me ask you a question. How do I deal with the anger that I have?"

I said, "Well, I can tell you that! For one thing, you come from an angry family. I have had to deal with a lot of anger, and you've heard about some of it. My father was very angry, his father was very angry, so you need to deal with this family spirit of anger."

He said, "Ok, I know how to do that."

I said, "Then we need to talk about balancing what your expectations are: what you are actually experiencing." We had a good discussion, which included all aspects of anger management.

Then I said, "While I am on this trip, I will ask the Lord if there is anything else you need to know about dealing with anger." Honestly, I did not think there was anything else. I had been counseling for years and I thought that was all there was to know. So, we left a few days later and flew to Europe.

About six weeks into our trip, I remembered what I'd said to my son. I wanted to be honest and truthful. So, I said, "Lord, is there anything You want to tell me about anger so I can tell Rick?" I was driving by myself in Portugal at the time.

Honestly, I did not expect the Lord to tell me anything. But He said, "Yes, you are angry because you judge."

I said, "I'm not talking about me. This is for my son."

He said, "You're angry because you judge."

I said, "No, it's not true. I'm a nice person and I do not get angry anymore. Lord, I was trained as a counselor, I was trained not to judge." (The Lord is never impressed with our reasons.)

He just kept saying, "You're angry because you judge."

Judgment

I said, "Ok Lord, I believe You, but I do not see how it's true. Will You show me?"

He said, "Gladly, I will show you."

> For the next thirty minutes, the Lord showed me what I had been doing in just the last four or five hours: I had been judging everybody! They drive fast and aggressively in Portugal. I was making judgments about everyone's driving.

I was sitting, waiting for a person to back out, so I could pull into a parking spot. But when they backed out, someone else pulled in front of me and into the space! I was so angry! They weren't waiting; I had been waiting for this spot. That is wrong; they are not supposed to do that!

The Lord said, "Ah, see there, judgment!"

I was shocked, as I recognized what was happening. I said, "Lord, I didn't realize I'd been doing this."

He said, "I know. I am showing you a new area in which I am going to set you free."

I said, "Ok Lord, I see it's wrong, I confess it to You, forgive me, and set me free." And then I made a mistake. I said, "God, I promise I won't do it anymore." Then it got worse. I would go back to the Lord and say, "Oh God, I'm doing it again. Forgive me."

It continued to get worse. Do you know why? I was using all of my will power to do the right thing, which made me subject to the law of sin. With my will, I would hold out and do the right thing until I ran out of will power.

Even when somebody would almost run me off the road, I'd say, "Bless them." But inside I would be thinking, "Oh, they are wrong! But I'm going to be a nice person and bless them, even though they're really wrong." Eventually, I would run out of will-power. Usually, when that happened, it would be some little, tiny thing, nothing big, just something tiny that would happen, and all of my anger would pour out.

What I remember was a little girl holding a door, and it slipped out of her hands and hit me in the face. I just blew up. I felt horrible; how could I do that?

God said, "Because you're judging."

I said, "Well, there seems to be a problem."

God said, "Yes, there is."

I said, "I do not want to do it anymore."

He said, "Quit doing it in your own strength."

I said, "What is the battle?"

He said, "The more that you know what is right, the more you will judge."

I said, "What?"

He said, "The person who doesn't know what is

right, does not judge anything. They do not care. The more you know what is right, the more you see when someone is violating what's right."

I said, "That doesn't seem fair to me."

God said, "No, it's not fair. You need my life and power not to judge; not more of your will-power."

While I was driving in Portugal, I learned to forgive all of these people. So, I said, "Ok, that means I'm not judging them now. Right?"

But, the Lord said, "No, you still judge them. You felt hurt by them, you forgave them, and you released them to me. But guess what? You still evaluated them and decided they were right or wrong, didn't you?"

I said, "I'd have to be dead not to do that! What am I supposed to do?"

He said, "Here are the steps to freedom; recognize it is your human nature to judge. Do not try to ignore it, do not try to pretend it is not there, and do not think that because you have forgiven it, that it is taken care of. Do not try to be religious and say, 'Oh God, I forgive them and bless them.' Instead, tell Me what you are judging them for and confess that it is sin. Remember, sin is not that you are just doing the wrong thing, it's the law and the condition of sin trying to destroy you and them. You need to say to Me, 'God, this is sin, I hate this! Lord, forgive me, cleanse me of this sin.' If you haven't forgiven others, forgive them. Then do one more thing. Bring that judgment to Me and say, 'Lord, I nail this judgment, that you paid for with Your blood, to the cross. I ask You to put this judgment to death, so Satan can't use the judgment against me to put me to death.'" (Colossians 2:13-15)

I said, "Wow! Is there anything else?"

He said, "Yes, offer yourself to me and say, 'Here I am, Your servant; cleanse me. Is there anything you want me to do or say to this person?'"

Most of the time God says, "No, be quiet." Sometimes He says, "Yes, show mercy." Then He pours the mercy into us to show to them. He may say, "Express compassion." If He tells us to act a particular way, if He says, "Show that act of love…" He may then ask us to be kind in a specific way so that it brings a sense of redemption to the other person.

I started practicing this new way of dealing with judgments, but I didn't tell my wife about this experience I had just had with God.

About a month later, I was driving to the northern part of Portugal with Donna sitting beside me. I had been driving for four hours when out of the corner of my eye, I saw Donna staring at me. You know how that works? I could see it and I could feel it. So, I said, "What?"

She said, "It's nothing."

I said, "It's something. It has to be something. I can see it in your eyes. You're looking at me."

She said, "Well, of course, I'm looking at you."

I said, "No, it's a particular look."

Finally, she said, "Well, I've just been wondering, what's happened to you?"

I said, "What do you mean?"

She said, "You're not as angry as you normally are."

I said, "What do you mean, normally angry?" But then I said, "Well, let me tell you what the Lord told me." I told her all about the experience with the Lord and the changes I had been making.

She just looked at me and said, "Well, it's working, keep it up."

A few weeks later, we met with Rick before returning home. I told him all that happened and what the Lord taught me.

He said, "Great Dad, I'll do it."

I said, "Wonderful."

> ## Signs we are judging
>
> How do you and I know if we are judging? Do you have hurt feelings, disappointments, frustrations, suspicions, bitterness, anger, condemnation, indignation, accusations, regrets or strong emotions?
> If we feel any of these, it means we are judging. It is human nature to judge. It happens automatically. We may think that we are just making an observation or asking questions to evaluate. We may say, "I'm just trying to investigate." But we are doing it so we can make a decision as to what is right or wrong.

| Image 5: Questions to Know We're Judging

For the next few months, God was showing me what was happening. I was still judging. So, I continued doing this process the Lord laid out for me. And I was feeling pretty good about the changes I was making.

Then Donna and I were to celebrate our twenty-fifth wedding anniversary. She had been planning it for about a year. We went to Hawaii and Donna said, "You have to promise that for the first two weeks you won't talk to anyone that we know in Hawaii."

I said, "What are we going to do?"

She said, "We are going to be together, just us."

I said, "Okay." So, we spent two weeks with just the two of us. And I walked on the beach. I drank coffee, we talked, we read, we slept, we talked more and at the end of two weeks I said, "It's time to connect with more people." As you can tell, I'm more of a people person than Donna.

She said, "Oh I could do this for another two months."

I was thinking, "Oh, I would die."

So, then we went to another island. There were two pastors and their wives that we knew, and I was going to be teaching in both churches. We stayed with one pastor and his wife, but the other pastor and his wife picked us up and took us out to dinner that night. Then they brought us back to where we were staying. When we opened the door and walked in, there was a wonderful aroma of Kona coffee. I really like Kona coffee and I could smell the coffee brewing.

The month before this, the Lord said to me, "Do not drink coffee or eat dessert until further notice." But I thought, "Well, I'm on vacation. She made the coffee just for me." Then I saw a cherry cheese-cake on the table. I really like this dessert; it is one of my favorites!

But you know how we can rationalize things. So, I automatically thought, "Well, I do not want her to feel bad. She made this just for me. She will be very disappointed if I do not eat or drink anything. So, I thought I could drink half a cup of coffee and eat half a piece of dessert. That would probably be okay with God. Right? I didn't think any more about it. I was enjoying our conversation together.

Eventually, our wives said, "It's late and we need to go to bed." They went to bed while the pastor and I stayed up and talked for another couple of hours. Finally, we said goodnight to each other, and went to bed.

Two hours later, I woke up. I had a painful stomach ache with increasing pain. I looked at the clock at the end of the bed and it was two o'clock in the morning. It did not occur to me about the cheese-cake and the coffee. I laid my hand on my stomach and said, "Lord, I thank You that through the blood of Jesus I have been healed. You took every wound on Your body. All of this pain, leave in the name of Jesus." The pain got worse. So, I rebuked that spirit of pain and infirmity, and it got worse. I thought, "Well, I may need to cancel some curse someone has pronounced toward me. So, I prayed and canceled any curse aimed at me. The pain intensified. It started moving up into my chest. I said, "Lord, I'm getting a little fearful. I rebuke that spirit of fear." The Lord didn't say anything. Suddenly, it felt like someone hit me in the chest with a hammer. All this pain shot down my left arm and I quit breathing. I said, "Lord, this feels like a spirit of death."

He said, "This is not a spirit. It is death."

All of this was happening instantaneously. I said, "Lord, You have my attention if You have anything You want to say."

The Lord said, "This is Satan trying to kill you."

I said, "What? How?"

He said, "He's using your judgments to try to put you to death."

I said, "What judgments? I've been doing everything You said to do."

And then He opened my mind and showed me what I'd just been doing for the last two hours. The other pastor and I had been talking about the church. Not just a particular congregation, but the church around the world.

The Lord said, "Look at all those judgments you made." He said, "That's My bride you were talking about." He said, "You cannot talk about her like that. All of those other servants of Mine you were talking about; they are Mine also."

I said, "Lord, forgive me, I repent." I was crying, I was repenting, and I was naming those judgments and nailing them to the cross. "Lord, You put them to death, not me." I watched the clock slowly ticking; I wasn't breathing for half an hour.

The Lord said to me, "I'm keeping you alive, with My grace and mercy."

Soon I started laughing and crying all at the same time because I was breathing again. The pain in my chest was gone, but the pain in my stomach remained. I was laughing and crying, but I didn't care. I was glad to be alive.

Meanwhile, Donna was still asleep. She slept through the whole thing. I decided to wake her up and have her pray for my stomach. I said, "Donna, my stomach hurts, would you pray for me?"

Donna doesn't wake up easily. Without even turning over, she laid her hand on my stomach and began to pray, "Oh Lord, what do you want to say about this?" She prayed in tongues and said, "I see a ring of fire; I see you walk into it, and you don't come out. I think God wants you to repent."

Then she went back to sleep, and I said, "Well, thank you very much! What kind of prayer is that?"

Then the Lord said to me, "What about the coffee and dessert?"

I said, "Oh God, I repent, forgive me Lord, cleanse me and set me free. Now Lord, you will take the pain away, right?"

He said, "No."

I said, "Yes! You have to."

He said, "No I don't."

"Well, Your Word said You will heal me."

Judgment

He said, "You are healed."

"But I still have pain."

He said, "You will have to walk through it."

And I said, "What? Okay, Lord."

So, I spent the next few hours in the bathroom repenting and praising the Lord. I was not going to tell anybody about this, and I was not going to tell Donna about what had happened. I thought what I experienced physically was just a spiritual experience. I got dressed and took an early morning walk. It was Sunday and I was scheduled to preach in about two hours.

I was about half-way through the message when I heard the Lord say to me, "Stop what you are saying and tell them what happened this morning."

But I continued to preach while having an internal conversation with the Lord. "No, I'm not going to say this. I'm not going to tell them."

The Lord said, "Stop what you're doing and tell them." You know, you can ignore the Lord and still do something religious? God said, "Stop what you're doing and tell them."

Finally, I obeyed and said, "Okay." Then I said, "I need to stop and tell you something."

Donna was sitting right there on the front row, and as I described my night, her eyes began to get really big. She said, "I sort of remember that part, but I didn't know all that was going on."

After I shared, everyone started crying. They

explained, "We've been having a judgment problem between our church and another church. We need to repent and nail our judgments to the cross, and then go over and talk with them." That is what they did. They went over to the other church and said, "We need to ask your forgiveness." It was so good to witness everyone repenting of their judgments and forgiving each other.

I discovered, for me, taking care of my judgments is a matter of life and death. What I thought was a spiritual experience, I discovered was also physical. Years later, my Cardiologist informed me that testing confirmed that I had had a heart attack. I have had other experiences with judgments as well, but they are too numerous to share here.

But what I can declare is: along with forgiving someone, and releasing them, it is also necessary to take our judgments to the Lord and nail them to the cross, so they can be put to death. Then Satan cannot use them against us to steal, kill, and destroy. And we can say with Jesus, "The ruler of this world is coming, but he has nothing in me." (John 14:30)

> One area of judgment that we often overlook is the judgment toward ourself. Other people may play into this, but the biggest hindrance to us is the area of questions we hear in our head that usually start with the words *what if*. If we ignore these or if we

entertain them, there is a negative judgment that fills us with more doubt and fear.

These *what if* questions actually come from Satan. His purpose is to have us agree and accept those conclusions, so that he can fulfill those judgments in our life. This is one of the ways he fulfills his plan to steal, kill and destroy us.

Here is a recap of what I learned about dealing with anger.

Steps to Freedom:

1. Recognize that it is human nature to judge.
2. Confess it as sin.
3. Receive forgiveness.
4. Forgive others.
5. Nail judgments to the cross.
6. Reckon yourself dead to sin and alive to God in Christ Jesus.

Colossians 2:13-15 "*And when you were dead in your transgressions and the uncircumcision of your flesh, He made you alive together with Him, having forgiven us all our transgressions. Having canceled out the certificate of death consisting of decrees against us which was hostile to us; and He has taken it out of the way, having nailed it to the cross. When He had disarmed the rulers and authorities, He made a public display of them, having triumphed over them through Him.*"

CHAPTER 3
SCRIPTURES TO KNOW

*H*ere are some scriptures you need to read and become acquainted. One of the things you learn in scripture, is that the only one that is supposed to judge is God, Himself. You also learn that God is no longer judging anything or anyone. He said He has appointed a day and a time to judge. When everything here on the earth is completed, then judgment will come.

Until then, *God is not judging*.

I was surprised by that. I had always heard that when someone does something wrong, and they are experiencing problems, it is the judgment of God. Have you heard something similar?

I asked God, "What about that?"

God said, "That is not Me judging. They are the natural consequences of what people do. My desire is to show them how to live freely and not be subject to the law."

From this conversation, I concluded that God is not saying, "Ok, based on the bad things you have done, I'm going to bring these bad things into your life to punish you." No, what He says is, "I am looking for a way to pour out mercy and grace to you because My Son, Jesus, already paid the price, when judgment happened on the cross."

I said, "This is very interesting."

God said, "When you are judging and you say it is Me, you are misrepresenting My nature to people. That is Satan's nature, not Mine."

> Matt. 7:1-2, *"Do not judge, lest you be judged, for in the way you judge, you will be judged, and by your standard of measure, it will be measured to you."*

> Matthew 7:3-5 *"Why do you look at the speck that is in your brother's eye, but do not notice the log that is in your own eye? Or how can you say to your brother, 'Let me take the speck out of*

your eye,' and behold the log is in your own eye? You hypocrite, first take the log out of your own eye, and then you will see clearly to take the speck out of your brother's eye."

Image 6: Matthew 7:3-5 Log in Your Eye

Luke 6:36-38 "Be merciful, just as your Father is merciful. And do not judge and you will not be judged; and do not condemn and you will not be condemned; pardon, and you will be pardoned. Give, and it will be given to you, good measure, pressed down, shaken together, running over, they will pour into your lap. For by your standard of measure it will be measured to you in return."

Image 7: Luke 6:36-38 Measured to You in Return

John 7:24 "Do not judge according to appearance, but judge with righteous judgment."

Judgment

Image 8: John 7:24 image - Do Not Judge By Looks… Ask God

Romans 2:1-6 "Therefore you are without excuse, every man of you who passes judgment, for in that you judge another, you condemn yourself; for you who judge practice the same things. And we know that the judgment of God rightly falls upon those who practice such things. And do you suppose this, oh man, when you pass judgment upon those who practice such things and do the same yourself, that you will escape the

35

judgment of God? Or do you think lightly of the riches of His kindness and forbearance and patience, not knowing that the kindness of God leads you to repentance? But because of your stubbornness and unrepentant heart, you are storing up wrath for yourself in the day of wrath and revelation of the righteous judgment of God, who will render to every man according to his deeds."

Image 9: Romans 2:16 God Will Judge the Secrets of Men

Romans 2:16 "On the day when, according to my gospel, God will judge the secrets of men through Christ Jesus."

Romans 14:1, 3-4 "Now accept the one who is weak in faith, but not for the purpose of passing judgment on his opinions."
"Let not him who eats regard with contempt him who does not, eat and let not him who does not eat judge him who eats, for God has accepted him. Who are you to judge the servant of another? To his own master he stands or falls; and stand he will, for the Lord is able to make him stand."

Image 10: Romas 14:1, 3-4 Who Are You to Judge the Servant of Another?

Romans 14:10-13 "But you, why do you judge your brother? Or you again, why do you regard your brother with contempt? For we shall all stand before the judgment seat of God. For it is written, 'As I live, says the Lord, every knee shall bow to Me, and every tongue shall give praise (confess) to God.' So then each one of us shall give account of himself to God. Therefore, let us not judge one another anymore, but rather determine this- not to put an obstacle or a stumbling block in a brother's way."

Image 11: Romans 14:10-13 Do Not Lay Out a Stumbling Block For Your Brother

I Corinthians 2:14-15 "But a natural man does not accept the things of the Spirit of God; for they are foolishness to him, and he cannot understand them, because they are spiritually appraised. But he who is spiritual appraises all things, yet he himself is appraised by no man."

Image 12: 1 Corinthians 2:14-15 Natural Man vs. Spiritual Man

James 2:12-13 "*So speak and so act, as those who are to be judged by the law of liberty. For judgment will be merciless to one who has shown no mercy; mercy triumphs over judgment.*"

James 4:10-12 "*Humble yourselves in the presence of the Lord, and He will exalt you. Do not speak against one another, brethren. He who speaks against a brother, or judges his brother, speaks*

against the law, and judges the law; but if you judge the law, you are not a doer of the law, but a judge of it. There is only one Lawgiver and Judge, and One who is able to save and to destroy; but who are you who judge your neighbor?"

James 5:9,12 "Do not complain, brethren, against one another, that you yourselves may not be judged; behold, the Judge is standing right at the door." "But above all, my brethren, do not swear, either by heaven or by earth, or with any other oath; but let your yes be yes and your no, no; so that you may not fall under judgment."

CHAPTER 4
THE BOOMERANG OF JUDGMENT

Through all of this, I learned that when I judge others, I am also judging the Judge. In essence, I am saying, "You are not doing Your job." That is not a good thing to do, is it? No! We don't realize we are attempting to take God's place and trying to do the Holy Spirit's function. We know this is impossible.

So, we see Satan trying to deceive us by subconsciously accusing others, and even God to us. If we receive his lies and act on them, we become the judge and give our judgment.

**But if we do, it boomerangs,
and those judgments happen to us instead.**

Satan and the world's system carry those judgments out upon us because we are out of place, and what we are giving is used as seed to produce more fruit in our lives. Unfortunately, it is the wrong fruit. It is the works of the flesh and not the fruit of the Spirit. In this way, Satan is able to steal, he is able to kill and he is able to destroy.

I saw that scripture says, "Who am I to judge the servant of someone else?" The servant is not my servant. He is a servant of the Lord. I am a servant of the Lord. Who am I to judge? It says, "Before his own master, he stands or falls." (Romans 14:4)

> Do you see why it is so important to learn to forgive and to take your judgments to the Judge, and nail them to the cross? We must have the Lord crush them and put them to death so they cannot be used as seed to steal, kill and destroy us? We want to experience life abundantly, as Jesus promised in John 10:10.

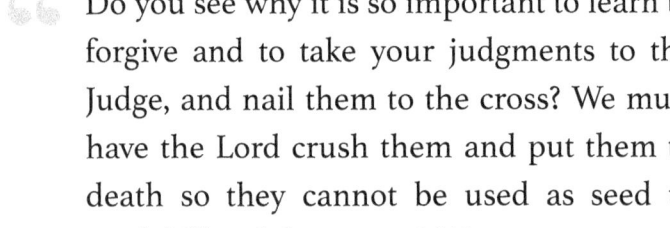

**I had an experience relating to this.
It was a little more involved.**

We were visiting Portugal for several weeks and we met a sweet young couple with whom we connected. He was an international football/soccer star. They asked us to

Judgment

stay with them for a few days. While we were there, another couple came over to thank them for helping them with moving expenses. I was in another room while the three-hour conversation was going on. It happened that other couple stayed for dinner. During dinner time, I began to feel very uneasy. I couldn't understand much of the Portuguese. But I began to feel disturbed about this relationship as I began to pray and intercede. As a result, I had a lot of judging going on within me about this man and his wife. (But I was not yet aware of it.)

The next day, Donna and I were to do an all-day marriage seminar. After the seminar, we were scheduled to go to a soccer game. It involved the European Cup and was an important game. I had been up all the night the night before, in the bathroom. I was not feeling well. Because of that, we were late arriving at the seminar. As soon as the seminar was over, a group of us piled into cars and caravanned to the soccer stadium.

The longer we sat at the game, the worse I felt. I was so sick I could not continue to sit there. Walking around did not help; nothing was comfortable. Finally, when the game was over, I could not drive home. I asked my long-time friend, Jim, if he would drive my rental car back to his house, where we were staying the next few days. He drove me back to his house.

When we arrived, it was ninety-eight degrees outside, but I was freezing cold. I put on a coat and wrapped myself in a blanket. I was shaking, all my color was gone, and I ached all over. We were staying in their downstairs apartment. I asked Donna if she would get Jim and his wife, Helen, and the two visiting American men to come and pray for me. They all came downstairs, and we spent the next two hours praying.

As they prayed, the Lord showed me three things:

1. A Christian man, without realizing it, had brought a curse upon my soccer friend. As I entered into an intercessory position (standing in the gap), this brought that curse upon me as well. And because of my judgment, I was taking the brunt of it. Also, my friend hadn't performed well in the soccer game. It looked like he was playing in slow motion. The next day, we found out he also felt sickly.
2. I realized it was Saturday night and that I was scheduled to preach Sunday morning. I knew that if I didn't feel better, I would not be able to preach. So, we continued praying. We cancelled the curse over my soccer friend that was affecting us both; and I nailed my judgments to the cross. We then pronounced God's blessing on all those involved. The effects of cancelling the curse and

pronouncing the blessing did not occur until my judgments were nailed to the cross. This was a new revelation to me!

3. Then the Lord showed me some people wanted us to stay in Portugal longer. As a matter of fact, they had prayed that something would happen so we couldn't go home. They were doing this out of their love for us, not with a bad motive. But because of the undealt with judgments on my part, Satan was able to use it to affect me physically and tried to fulfill their desires by negative means. Means that are contrary to God's will and purpose for our lives.

I used to just laugh at that kind of thing, but I began to realize that as Christians, God's power is at work within us.

> If what we are wishing and desiring is contrary to God's purpose, it may be used to try to block what God is doing in the spiritual realm and then affect the physical.

So, we prayed, and I started to feel a little better.

God said, "Oh by the way, let me show you all of your judgments that you have not dealt with recently."

I said, "Oh God, not again."

Then He began to uncover things I had said that were subtle, small things. I had been dealing with the obvious ones, but I had not recognized those subtle judgments that I was making about this person and that person. So, I took this to the Lord also.

You know what? As soon as that happened, my temperature changed, all the pain left, and blood came back into my face. I got really hot, took off all the blankets and the coat I was wearing, got out of bed and suddenly realized I was hungry.

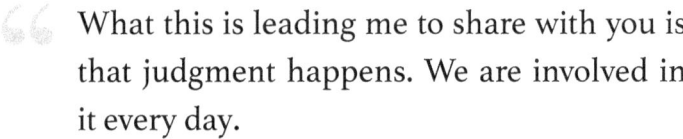
> What this is leading me to share with you is that judgment happens. We are involved in it every day.

The ruler of this world has been judged by God and because He has come to this world, judgment has come. It is what Satan does. But now, God is redeeming us from judgment by offering mercy and grace. Either we can deal with all this judgment now and take it before God, or we can face it later. What I am saying is that I do not want to face it later. I thank God that Jesus took care of it on the cross and we can appropriate His grace now.

Image 13: God is The Father and The Judge

As I prayed, "Father, I don't want to give judgment to anyone else. I don't want them to have to experience my judgments. I want Your blessing to come into their lives." I began to realize there were times God wanted me to speak to someone in a very firm way, but I would not do it because of my judgment. Judgment is not only directed against people; it may also prevent us from functioning in the Spirit of the Lord.

I found there were times I would take my judgments to God, He put those to death and cleansed me. Then He would tell me to do something. But I would say, "That sounds harsh. I don't want to tell them that. I would never say that to them."

The Lord said, "Listen, it is not you who are telling them. I want to tell them through you. Go tell them what I said!"

When I obeyed, and gave the other people the words God had given me, it sounded too harsh. But they would receive it. The difference was they did not taste my judgment. They did not taste anything of me, instead God's words set them free. Instead of receiving destructive consequences for eternity, they received revelation of God's mercy and grace.

CHAPTER 5
ACTION STEPS TO FREEDOM

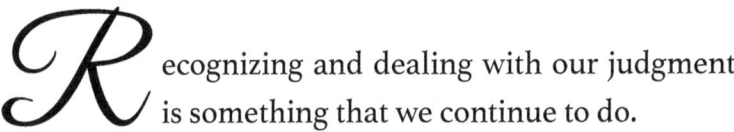ecognizing and dealing with our judgment is something that we continue to do.

It is not a one-time thing!

Working through our judgments with the Lord, will eventually rewire and transform the way we think, allowing God to show His love to others through our words and actions.

As you begin to exercise these things and make them part of your daily prayer and interaction with the Lord, He will work in you to bring freedom and transformation that allows you to love others as Christ loves them.

Image 14: Steps to Freedom

What are we to do?

1. Offer yourself to God.
2. Forgive and release others and yourself.
3. Nail your judgments to the cross so they can be put to death.
4. Reckon yourself as dead to sin and alive to God.
5. Ask the Holy Spirit to cleanse you.
6. Ask God if there is anything He wants you to do or say.
7. Show mercy.
8. Express compassion.

9. Act out of love.
10. Offer redemption.

**Interact with God!
Make this prayer your own.**

> Lord, I offer myself to You as Your child, for Your purpose. And I forgive _____ for _____. They are not accountable to me. I forgive myself for judging them. It is now between You and them. It is under The Blood of Christ. I take all my judgments of _____ and nail them to the cross. You put them to death there, so that Satan cannot use them to put me to death. I reckon myself as dead to sin and its destruction. And I reckon myself as alive in Christ with eternal resurrection life. Holy Spirit, come and cleanse me and fill me with Your Life and Power. Father God, what would You like to do or say through me towards this person? Thank You, Lord, for setting me free to show mercy, love, and to be a blessing. Amen!

ABOUT THE AUTHOR

Dick Sorenson was born in Twin Falls, Idaho, in 1946. When he was one day old, he was adopted into a loving non-Christian family and raised as an only child. At the age of three, his family moved to Nevada, where he grew up in the rough and tumble "wild west" environment for 10 years before moving back to Idaho.

Dick experienced a life changing encounter with Jesus Christ while reading the Gospels. He accepted Jesus as his Savior and was born again. A few weeks later, on Easter Sunday, he was baptized in water. It was also his 15th birthday. Two years later, he had another course-altering encounter that lead him to give up two college scholarships, one in nuclear physics and one in wrestling, to pursue full-time ministry. Then a scholarship was offered for him to attend Central Christian College of the Bible in Moberly, Missouri. He studied Hebrew for one year and studied Greek for three years. He furthered his education at Eastern New Mexico University, in Portales, New Mexico, receiving a double Master's Degree in Counseling and Theology. At age 20, Dick planted two new churches while still in college.

Since giving his life to full-time ministry since 1966, God has worked through him in resolving church conflicts, helping churches understand Biblical leadership, imparting vision, and as a resource for pastors and missionaries. In 1974, he started one of the first Christian Counseling practices in the State of Idaho, which served the community for 15 years. Traveling internationally since 1983, including ministry to unreached people groups, he has ministered in over 100 countries, training leaders and conducting seminars around the world. His non-denominational approach has reached across denominational lines, resulting in many lives touched through teaching, counseling, prayer and deliverance ministry.

Dick has a heart for the Nations and the workers in the field, taking teams for work projects, teaching the Word and prayer-walking in restricted access areas of the world. His passion is to prepare and urge people to step out in the call God has for them. He sits on three ministry boards and currently resides in Boise, Idaho, with his wife Donna, who he has been happily married to for over 55 years. They have two married children, two married grandsons and two great-granddaughters.

Dick and Donna live to fellowship—
anywhere, anytime, and over coffee
preferably!

MORE TOPICS IN THIS SERIES

Titles in this series: 13

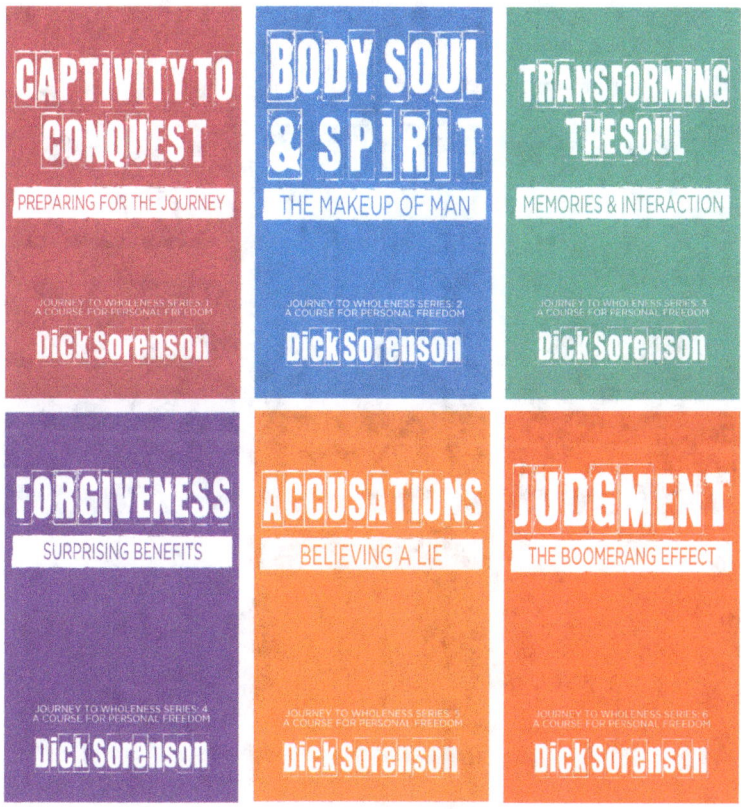

Titles 1-6 in Journey to Wholeness Series

Titles 7-13 in Journey to Wholeness Series

Journey to Wholeness Series

1. Captivity to Conquest - *Preparing for the Journey*
2. Body, Soul & Spirit - *The Makeup of Man*
3. Transforming the Soul - *Memories & Interaction*
4. Forgiveness - *Surprising Benefits*
5. Accusations - *Believing a Lie*
6. Judgment - *The Boomerang Effect*
7. Brokenness - *Identifying Bruises and Wounds*
8. Healing of the Soul - *God's Intention*
9. Vows & Curses - *From Chains to Blessings*
10. Pulling Down Strongholds - *A Personal Privilege*
11. Binding the Strongman - *God Initiated Encounter*
12. Deliverance - *Steps to Freedom*
13. Areas of Spiritual Warfare - *Using the Right Tools*

The first six booklets in this series are centered on repairing, restoring, healing, and transforming areas of our past.

As we move on through the next 7 booklets, we'll be breaking free and rebuilding, replacing lies with truth, standing against the attacks of the enemy, pulling down strongholds, and we will be setting free what is bound.

That's good! It's not something we do just once; it's a lifestyle we learn to live with. Because of the rebellion, and the result of war Satan started in heaven, and brought to earth, you and I are in spiritual warfare.

We will talk about spiritual warfare, look at the overview and then go over what is happening up close and personal in our lives.

About this Series

The *Journey to Wholeness* series is designed to be used as a guide or study to bring an individual into personal freedom and spiritual maturity. It is also designed to use as a study guide for a small gathering, home group, or a classroom setting. This material is a resource for leading a discipleship group, personal growth group, or teaching a series for ministry training. Each topic is a separate booklet. Although all topics fit together to become the *Journey to Wholeness*, each can be discovered and applied separately to impart life, freedom, and spiritual growth as needed.

The way this series became available is rather unique since every single word in these booklets was spoken. The contents of this series have been compiled from PowerPoint slides, the seminar workbook, and transcribed audio recordings on wholeness Dick delivered at a training center in Cairo, Egypt. This series is an original course of Dick Sorenson Ministries.

Hiking toward hope on a personal journey to wholeness…

Thank you for your participation in this series.

If you've gained insight, we invite you to share your thoughts. You can do this in several ways:

- Leave a review
- Share on social media using the hashtags #j2wSeries, #dicksorenson, #thelanyaplifebooks and tagging us @thelanyaplife
- Contact us through our website thelanyaplife.com

SPECIAL THANKS

Many thanks to all those who have prayed, contributed to, and encouraged us to complete this series. We could not have accomplished this without your help.

May God bless you on your journey...

Donna Sorenson...
You are the one who made it happen. Your love and vision prompted each of us to see the importance of transferring "what was in Dick's head" to words on paper. You are the strength and spark...

Tami Sorenson Gaupp...
Our daughter was an answer to our prayers for help. We value her encouragement and push – she took this project from a seminar format to a booklet series by her persistence in learning new things... setting up a publishing company, book design and publishing.

Rick Sorenson...
Our son spent countless hours and days interacting with Dick, sorting out the life-application of each subject while applying them personally and giving feedback... always over a good cup of coffee.

Becky Hansen...
Her design skills have been an invaluable asset as she created and recreated diagrams and a cover... with laughter, sometimes tears, but always with patience for us.

Pam Pearson...
Who patiently spent day after day transcribing the recordings from Dick's teaching in Egypt the old-fashioned way –listen, stop, type, repeat...

Cindy Anderson...
Was part of the initial work to get us started, using her writing skills in outlining and putting a structure to this material...

Fount Shults...
Gave his time to Dick, studying and engaging in endless hours of fruitful discussion...

What a blessing you all are to us...

OTHER BOOKS

The Season of 2s & 3s: take the experiment and see what God does —by Dick Sorenson

We are called to be the Lord's ambassadors and to be more than conquerors in the dominion of darkness. This call will affect history and bring about God's purposes. But we do not do the work, God does, and He will use the agreement of just 2 or 3 to bring it about.

Other Books

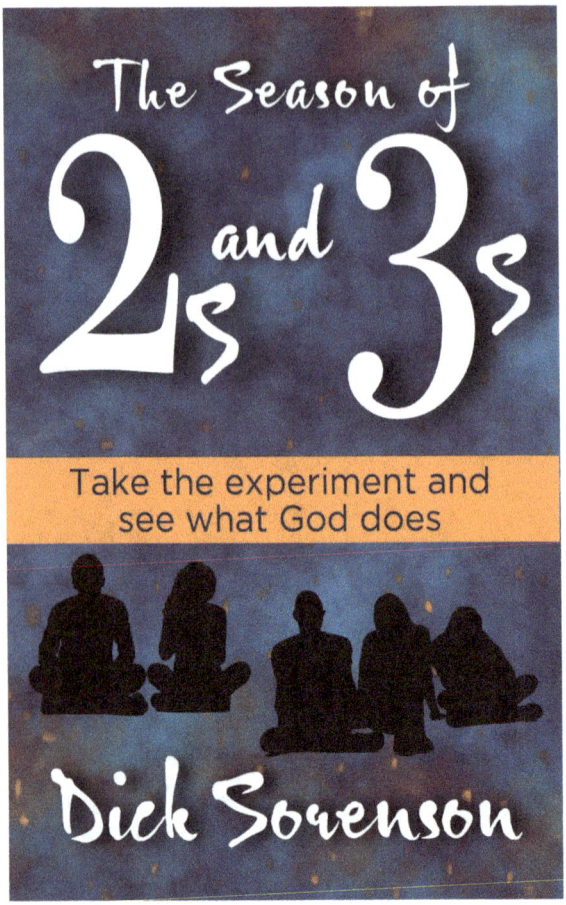

Dick Sorenson gives a powerful account of an experience he had over 30 years ago and shares how God is bringing it all together with past and present visions to let us know the time is now.

See. Hear. Do. Prayer: 8-week kickstart to a new prayer life— by Tami Sorenson Gaupp

Prayer doesn't look the same for everyone. Find out how to make your prayer life an adventure! In *See. Hear. Do. Prayer, y*ou'll be led to the heart of God, as Tami takes you on an adventure through this 8-week kickstart in prayer.

Other Books

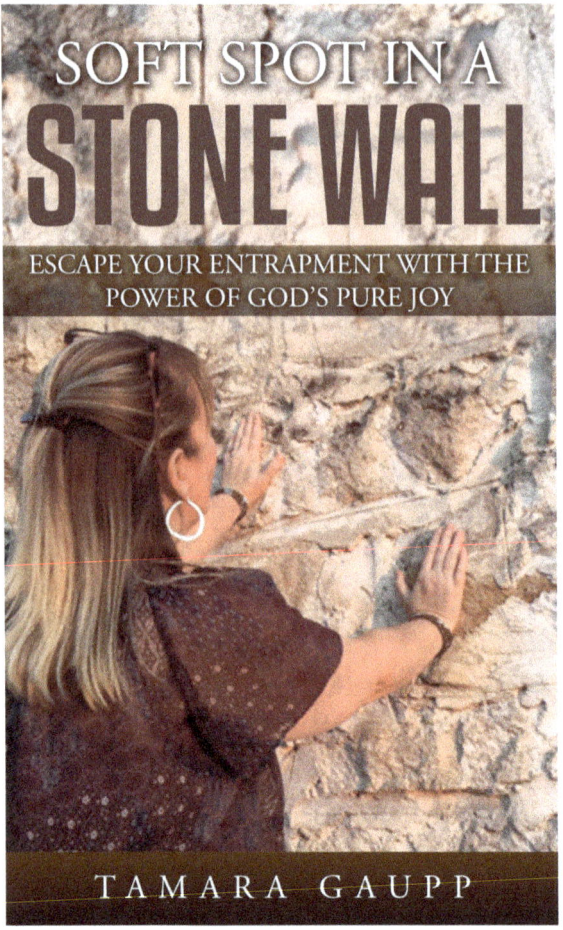

Soft Spot in a Stone Wall: Escape Your Entrapment with the Power of God's Pure Joy— by Tamara (Tami) Sorenson Gaupp

Soft Spot in a Stone Wall is about those areas in life we are not able to overcome. They may even feel like stone walls built up around us, holding us captive. These are the walls that ONLY the Almighty God has the power to break down. When we come to the end of ourselves, throw our troubles down at His feet, and cry out to Him to lead us out of our desperation, He opens a way before us, creating a soft spot that wasn't there before.

ww.thelanyaplife.com/books

www.ingramcontent.com/pod-product-compliance
Lightning Source LLC
Chambersburg PA
CBHW072106110526
44590CB00018B/3339